CREEPY CHRONICLES

Wicked Waters

Written by Barbara Cox and Scott Forbes

Gareth Stevens
Publishing

CONTENTS

What was that? It looked like a giant snake swimming in the water! Was it a ferocious sea serpent? Or maybe it was just a figment of your imagination.

You may never know. There are plenty of mysterious creatures lurking in the waters around the world. Deadly sea monsters, sinister goblins, colossal squids, scary ghost ships, and deceitful mermaids have made the bravest sailors question if they were fact or fiction. Most people think they're not real, so you aren't really afraid to go back in the water. Well . . . maybe you should be.

WICKED WATERS

LOCH NESS MONSTER

LOCH NESS MONSTER

OTHER NAMES: Nessie.

FACT OR FICTION: Scientists say fiction, but many people claim to have seen the monster and there are also photographs in existence (see opposite page).

DESCRIPTION: A huge serpentine creature with a long neck and a small head. It is about 30 feet (9 m) long in total and has at least one hump. It looks very much like a dinosaur, and many people believe that it might be a descendant of a dinosaur and has lived quietly in Loch Ness for millions of years.

WHERE THEY LIVE: Loch Ness—a large lake in Scotland.

POWERS: No magical powers, but due to its immense size, it's strong enough to overpower smaller creatures.

WEAKNESSES: It is obviously shy since it is rarely seen. It has only been seen in Loch Ness, so it probably cannot travel further.

DIET: By all accounts the Loch Ness Monster is a carnivore, meaning that it eats meat—it has been seen with smaller creatures in its mouth.

THE LOCH NESS MONSTER is a creature that is said to live in the huge lake called Loch Ness in Scotland. Although scientists dismiss it as a hoax or a figment of the imagination, there are many supposed sightings of the creature both in the water and on land. Some think it is a dinosaur.

SIGHTINGS

Loch Ness is a large lake in Scotland—23 miles (37 km) wide and 755 feet (230 m) deep. Throughout history, there have been legends of a Loch Ness Monster, and since the twentieth century there have been many sightings and photographs of "Nessie."

Possibly the first report of the monster was by Saint Columba. He met the monster on land, near the loch. It followed him but didn't dare attack because it recognized that he was a holy man.

That happened in the seventh century. Across the centuries that followed, there have been many stories about the beast. In 1933, a Mr. Spicer wrote to a London newspaper saying that he and his wife had been on holiday near Loch Ness and had seen a creature like "a dragon or a prehistoric animal," crossing the road in front of their car with a smaller animal in its mouth.

PHOTOGRAPHS

The first photographs of the monster date from the 1930s, showing it swimming with its head held above the water and with what seem to be humps on its back. Many other eyewitnesses have seen something similar, either in the loch or walking clumsily near the shore. However, numerous scientific tests and expeditions have all failed to come up with any proof of Nessie's existence.

LAKE MONSTERS

Nessie is typical of the lake monsters that appear in local legends all over the world. Some 250 lakes have stories of similar beasts, and these lakes are quite similar—all are large and very deep, and the water in them is always cold. Also, they all either connect with the sea or used to do so in earlier times.

No bodies or remains of the monsters have ever been found, and no live monsters have ever been caught. Nets and traps have been set, underwater cameras used, and teams of scientists have kept 24-hour watch for months without seeing anything. Yet people keep seeing strange creatures around these lakes.

MANIPOGO

A sociable monster that lives in Lake Manitoba.

The Manipogo, the monster that has been seen in Lake Manitoba in Canada, has been described as a huge brown snake with a long head like that of a horse or a sheep. Once, three Manipogos were observed swimming around together—they were seen by a group of 17 eyewitnesses.

FLATHEAD LAKE MONSTER

A many-humped monster that lives in Flathead Lake.

The monster in Flathead Lake in Montana has been described as being like a giant eel, swimming in an undulating movement that gives the impression of a series of humps. It is blackish in color, very shiny, and has a round head. It was first reported in 1889 and has been seen regularly since, usually during the spring and summer months.

SILVER LAKE: A MONSTER HOAX

In the 1850s, there was great excitement about a giant serpent which appeared in Silver Lake in New York. People traveled miles to see it and the area became busy and prosperous. But then there was a fire in the local hotel, after which firemen discovered in an attic room the remains of a wire and canvas model of a huge snake. The hotel owner had faked the whole thing to bring more business to his hotel.

Storsjön Creature

A lake monster from northern Sweden.

For more than 350 years, there have been stories of a huge creature living in Lake Storsjön in northern Sweden. A scientific society exists to investigate life-forms in the lake. According to eyewitnesses, the Storsjön Creature seems to be very like the one from Loch Ness, but is described as having a yellow underbelly.

White River Monster

A large beast that lives in White River, Arkansas.

There have supposedly been monsters in the White River since before the Civil War. One has certainly been reported recently, and eyewitnesses said it was very big and a grayish color with peeling skin. It can walk, and it has left huge footprints on the river bank.

Slimy Slim

A serpentine lake monster, also known as Sharlie.

Payette Lake in Idaho is in the mountains and surrounded by forests. Occasional monster stories have been heard over the last 15 years about this quiet lake, and interestingly, the reports are getting more frequent, so the monster is either getting bolder or more careless. The creature has been nicknamed Slimy Slim or Sharlie, and is said to be serpent-like in appearance with a head like that of a crocodile.

Right: Storsjön Creature depicted on a large rune stone.

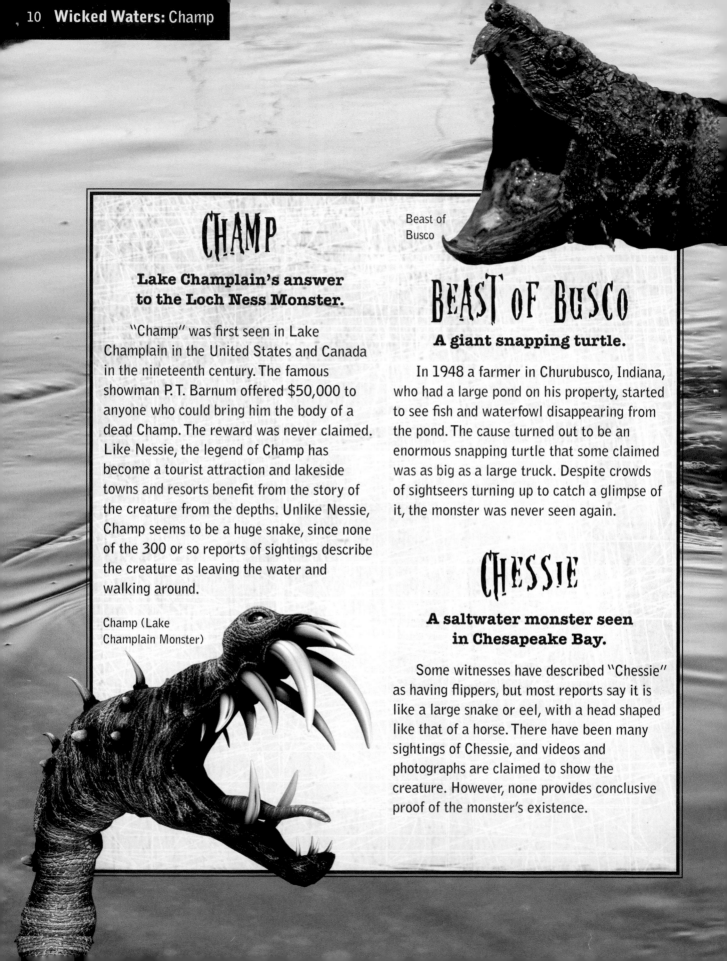

CHAMP

Lake Champlain's answer to the Loch Ness Monster.

"Champ" was first seen in Lake Champlain in the United States and Canada in the nineteenth century. The famous showman P. T. Barnum offered $50,000 to anyone who could bring him the body of a dead Champ. The reward was never claimed. Like Nessie, the legend of Champ has become a tourist attraction and lakeside towns and resorts benefit from the story of the creature from the depths. Unlike Nessie, Champ seems to be a huge snake, since none of the 300 or so reports of sightings describe the creature as leaving the water and walking around.

Champ (Lake Champlain Monster)

Beast of Busco

BEAST OF BUSCO

A giant snapping turtle.

In 1948 a farmer in Churubusco, Indiana, who had a large pond on his property, started to see fish and waterfowl disappearing from the pond. The cause turned out to be an enormous snapping turtle that some claimed was as big as a large truck. Despite crowds of sightseers turning up to catch a glimpse of it, the monster was never seen again.

CHESSIE

A saltwater monster seen in Chesapeake Bay.

Some witnesses have described "Chessie" as having flippers, but most reports say it is like a large snake or eel, with a head shaped like that of a horse. There have been many sightings of Chessie, and videos and photographs are claimed to show the creature. However, none provides conclusive proof of the monster's existence.

OGOPOGO

Canada's best-known lake monster.

Lake Okanagan in British Columbia is a long, narrow, and deep lake very similar to Loch Ness in Scotland. It has its own monster, known as Ogopogo. The most common description of the monster is that it is a serpent, 15 to 20 feet (5 to 6 m) long with a horse-like or sheep-like head.

The legend of a monster living in this lake goes back for centuries, and there have been many sightings. Originally the monster was known as Natiaka (from a Native American word meaning "lake demon").

One eyewitness account was from 1926. A couple driving past the lake on a very mild day saw the calm lake rippling and looked to see what was causing the movement. They spotted a large, strange-looking animal.

Some experts believe that these serpent-like monsters are a kind of primitive whale, or they may be a variety of sturgeon—a fish that can reach a great size and a great age.

THE DEVIL'S FOOTPRINTS

In February 1855, deep snow lay over the county of South Devon in England. One morning, residents awoke to find a trail of large hoof-prints in the snow, continuing across the countryside for some 60 miles (95 km) and going straight across roofs, walls, and other obstacles. At one point, the prints went down to the estuary of the Exe River and then began again on the other side of the river. As the Devil was believed to have cloven hooves, there were soon stories that he had been seen in person. The tracks never appeared again and have never been explained.

KAPPA

KAPPAS are water goblins that live in rivers and lakes in Japan. They are shaped like humans and are about the size of a nine-year-old child. With scaly skin, they are green, yellow, or occasionally blue in color and have webbed hands and feet.

WATER CHILDREN

Kappas, also known as "water children," are not very nice. They cause mischief, entice people into rivers to drown, and are said to kidnap and eat children. In spite of their small size, they're strong and can swim well. They can drag large animals into the water, hold them under, and drown them, which is something they like to do. They are particularly fond of attacking horses.

They are really best avoided, but, like many supernatural creatures, they have certain aspects that you can use to your advantage if you have to deal with one.

For example, you can buy them off with gifts —they like cucumbers, apparently.

Kappas are said to have a special hole in the top of their heads that contains magical water, which they carry with them when away from water. However, Kappas are also very interested in good manners. So if you meet a Kappa, it's wise to bow very deeply. The Kappa will return the bow, and the water will run out. The Kappa will then lose its power and be unable to move, allowing you to get away safely. Or you could refill the cavity with water, and then the Kappa would have to serve you for eternity.

KELPIE

A magical and dangerous water spirit that looks like a horse.

Kelpies are murderous water-spirits that live in rivers in Scotland and Ireland. A Kelpie usually takes the form of a handsome black horse. It will encourage you to pat it and then to ride it, but once on its back, you will be unable to jump off again. It will gallop into the water with you, pull you down to the depths, and eat you. They like to prey on children in particular.

Sometimes a Kelpie will turn itself into a beautiful woman with long black hair and will make a man fall in love with her, but the end of the story will be the same—he'll drown and be eaten.

It may be useful to know that Kelpies are always very cold to the touch, unlike real horses and women.

POOKA

A shape-shifting trickster spirit that can be deceitful.

Pookas, or Púcas, live around rivers in Scotland, Ireland, and also Wales. They can turn themselves into almost any kind of animal, such a wild horse, but will always have dark fur. They're tricky and like to entice you to go for a ride on their back, but, unlike the Kelpie, a Pooka will do you no real harm. They like to deceive and worry humans, and can be destructive if angered, but they can also be friendly and give good advice if treated with respect.

Below: Kelpies take the form of horses or beautiful women.

Ahuitzotl

AHUITZOTL

A nasty water monster from Aztec mythology, the Ahuitzotl lives in rivers in Mexico and Guatemala. It's like a cross between a smooth-haired black dog and a monkey. It has powerful arms and hands and an extra hand at the end of its long tail, which is useful for pulling its victims down into the water. It likes to eat people, especially the eyes, nails, and teeth.

CATOBLEPAS

An African monster that kills with a look, the Catoblepas lives in Ethiopia. It's a large, hairy, buffalo-like creature which carries its head low and looks at the ground. This is a good thing, because if it raises its head and looks straight at you, you will be turned to stone. Its breath can also kill you.

TARASQUE

There has only ever been one Tarasque, which came out of the Rhône River in Provence, France. It had six feet, a turtle-type shell on its back and a lion's head. It terrorized the region around the river until it was tamed by Saint Martha. Unfortunately, the local people didn't realize that it had been tamed, and they killed it. They then regretted what they had done and named their town Tarascon in its memory.

Model of the Tarasque in Tarascon, France.

REVENGE OF THE MULDJEWANGK

A Muldjewangk is a creature from Australian Aboriginal mythology. It was a huge monster—half-man, half-fish—which lived in the Murray River in South Australia. A Muldjewangk once attacked a steamboat that was owned by Europeans but had some Aboriginal elders on board. As the Muldjewangk's two enormous hands appeared and took hold of the side of the deck, the captain reached for his gun. The elders warned him not to shoot, but he did. The monster went away, but the captain fell ill with terrible blisters all over his body and died in agony six months later.

BUNYIP

The Bunyip is a mysterious creature that is said to occur all over Australia, and is mentioned in the myths of the ancient Dreamtime of the Aboriginal people. It supposedly lives in riverbeds, creeks, or other watery places.

There are many different descriptions of a Bunyip. Some say it's shaggy with a long tail. Others describe it as dog-faced. Some say it has claws and scaly skin like a crocodile, while others report it as having four paws.

What is certain is that a Bunyip lives in or near water and will kill and eat people. All descriptions agree that it has a loud, bellowing cry, which is frightening to hear and serves as a good warning to keep away from the area.

RUSALKA

**A beautiful and deadly
water ghost.**

A Rusalka is the ghost of a young woman
or child who has died by drowning. Most
Rusalkas were girls who committed suicide
because they were betrayed by a lover. They
haunt the river where they died (usually in
Russia or Poland). They sit by the side of the
river in a tree, dance hypnotically in a
water-meadow, or sing beautifully on the
river bank. But they are bitter, and their aim
is to capture young men and drown them.

BÄCKAHÄST

The Bäckahäst ("brook horse") is very
like a Kelpie, except that it's usually
a white horse and appears from the
river in foggy weather. To prey on people in
boats, it can disguise itself as an upturned
boat or a floating log until it gets near to its
victims. Then it will surge up out of the
water, seize them, and drag them down to
the depths. It also plays the same trick as
the Kelpie, appearing on land as a handsome
white horse and persuading unsuspecting
children to ride it. Whichever method it
uses, the Bäckahäst's aim in life is to
drown people and then eat them.

Anyone who climbs on the back of a Bäckhäst
will never be able to get off again.

NIX

A NIX is a water sprite, usually the spirit of a river. There are both male and female Nixes. The female is sometimes called a Nixie. These spirits can appear in human form, as a merman/mermaid with a fishy tail, or as some other animal or fish.

DANGEROUS BEAUTIES

Nixes often take the form of either beautiful or old women, and can also become invisible. In many German and Scandinavian folktales, seeing or hearing a Nix is a sign of danger and death.

Nixes often use song to lure fishermen and sailors into danger. The Lorelei was a famous example. She would sit on a rock in the Rhine River and sing to the boatmen, who would follow her beautiful voice and steer to their deaths on the dangerous rocks nearby. Nixes appear to do things like this purely for their own amusement.

Like other sinister elves and fairies, Nixes are indifferent to human happiness and can drive a hard bargain. There are stories where a Nix seems friendly and does a favor for a human, but then demands a child in payment. Nixes are said to live in underwater palaces, and it is possible to get on their good side by bribing them with gifts.

Some people believe that a Nix takes its power, and even its life, from its particular river, and if held captive on land, it will fade away and die.

As well as loving music and dancing, Nixes are thought to be able to tell the future.

SEA SERPENT

SEA SERPENT

OTHER NAMES: Sea monster.

FACT OR FICTION: Fiction but possibly some sightings were of real, oversized sea creatures, such as an oarfish.

DESCRIPTION: Generally like giant, scaly snakes, up to hundreds of feet long and up to 20 feet (6 m) thick, with heads that are like those of dragons or horses. Some have humps on their back. Some have been said to have hair, shells, eyes that shine, and sometimes a horse-like mane.

WHERE THEY LIVE: In the seas and oceans all around the world.

POWERS: Their enormous size and strength makes them very powerful.

WEAKNESSES: Their immense size may make them a little slow-moving. They can only live in water.

DIET: Fish and bigger marine creatures such as seals and whales. Sometimes human sailors become part of their diet, too!

A SEA SERPENT is a huge and dangerous creature seen in oceans in many parts of the world. Often hundreds of feet long, these giant sea snakes can attack ships at sea, overturning the boats easily with their huge and powerful bodies. Some people think that sea serpents are probably only whales or other huge fish.

SERPENTS OR FISH?

In the days when a sea voyage could last for years and ships navigated by the stars through uncharted waters, many sailors told tales of giant sea serpents that they'd seen in the far oceans. Like the lake monsters—the Loch Ness Monster and others—the sea serpents had humps on their backs, an undulating movement when swimming, and bony dragon-like or horse-like heads. They would be seen chasing and eating seals, small whales, and even sharks. The sea serpents were big—so big that any sailors who saw one were worried that it might attack them and cause their ship to overturn.

Modern scientists have suggested that the sea serpents may have been very large sturgeon, or possibly oarfish. Sturgeon are long thin fish that have the right shape of head, but, although big, they are not monster-sized. Oarfish are like enormous eels that live at the bottom of the ocean and are very seldom seen. They can grow to at least 15 feet (5 m) long, but even this is considerably smaller than the sea serpents sighted by sailors in the past. Also, oarfish don't have the distinctive "dragon-like" head so often described.

THE S.S. *TRESCO* AND THE SEA SERPENT

Joseph Grey, Second Officer of the S.S. *Tresco*, told how, in May 1903 in the South Atlantic, the crew saw a number of sharks swimming past at great speed as if escaping from danger. They then saw something in the water in the direction the sharks had come from.

As it came nearer, the sailors could see that it was a huge serpent, about 100 feet (30 m) long, with a narrow, bony head held up out of the water on a long neck. The sailors were terrified that it would attack the *Tresco* or collide with it. Grey claimed that the creature came near enough so that they could even see drool dripping from its mouth before it suddenly turned and swam away.

Most people who read the article thought that Grey had simply invented a colorful tale. But then the log of the SS *Tresco* was discovered. (A ship's log must be an accurate account of everything that happens on board.) It had this entry for May 30, 1903, at 10 a.m.: "Passed school of sharks followed by a huge sea monster."

KRAKEN

A KRAKEN is an enormous and aggressive squid that lives at the bottom of the sea. It can attack boats and ships, wrapping its huge tentacles around them and dragging them underwater.

FICTION AND FACT

Sailors in the olden days told tales of the Kraken, a huge octopus or squid, which would surge up from the depths of the ocean, grab onto a ship using the suckers on its many arms, and pull the vessel and everybody on board it down under the water. It would attack without warning and chances of survival for the sailors were slim. The Kraken, thought to be a typical sailors' legend like the mermaid, was said to live in the ocean off the coasts of Norway and Iceland.

Remarkably, we now know that real Krakens exist, although at the other end of the world. The colossal squid (Latin name *Mesonychoteuthis hamiltoni*) has only been known to scientists since 1925. It lives in the deepest water of the Antarctic seas and mature specimens grow to over 40 feet (12 m) long. Colossal squids have hooks on their eight arms as well as suckers, and are quite strong enough to pull a ship underwater. They are rare creatures and are seldom seen in shallow water; they have complex brains and experts say they are probably highly intelligent. During the 1930s there were three reported cases of colossal squids attacking ships.

LEVIATHAN

Leviathan is an enormous sea monster that is mentioned several times in the Bible. In the Book of Job, the creature is described as being monstrously huge and having terrifying large teeth and scales. It is also said to be able to breathe fire and deflect weapons such as spears. People often think that Leviathan was probably just a huge whale or maybe even a giant crocodile, but what is certain is that it lived in the ocean, not in a river. Often any large sea creature sighted today is referred to as a Leviathan.

Below: Leviathan is often thought to look something like a huge crocodile.

LUSCA

The sea around the islands of the Bahamas is famous for "blue holes"—deep pools and underwater caves that glow blue because of certain minerals in the rocks.

Unfortunately, these beautiful depths are also the home of the Lusca, which is half-shark and half-octopus. Many Bahamians believe that the creature will attack and kill unwary swimmers and divers.

SEA APE

Only one person has ever seen the Sea Ape—the explorer Georg Steller in 1741 near the Shumagin Islands in Alaska. Steller described it as being around 5 feet (1.5 m) long, having a dog-like head with pointed ears that stuck upwards and whiskers, a shark-like tail, grayish fur on its back, but reddish fur on its belly. The way that it rose up out of the water and watched the boat, and its agility, made Steller believe it was some kind of ape. However, it's more likely to have been a seal, especially due to the description of the color, ears, and whiskers.

SCYLLA

SCYLLA was an enormous Greek sea monster with six heads who lurked in a cave, waiting for unsuspecting ships to pass by. She would then attack, devouring anyone who might be on board.

SIX HEADS

In ancient Greek mythology, Scylla was an immortal and deadly sea monster with six heads, each of which had four eyes and three rows of extremely sharp teeth. She (the monster is female, apparently) also had twelve tentacles instead of legs, and, in some stories, had more toothy heads attached at waist level, which were like the heads of vicious dogs. Scylla waited on the rocks for ships to come near enough for her to snatch the sailors and devour them.

BEAUTY AND BEAST

According to the ancient Roman writer Ovid, Scylla was originally a beautiful nymph. One day she was seen by the sea god Glaucus, and he fell in love with her. However, Scylla did not return his affection, and she ran from him onto land where he could not follow. Wishing to find a spell to make her fall in love with him, Glaucus sought out the witch, Circe. Unfortunately, Circe fell in love with Glaucus and decided to get rid of Scylla. She transformed the nymph into the sea monster.

CHARYBDIS

Another ancient Greek monster of the sea who creates dangerous whirlpools.

Charybdis is an evil monster who can create powerful and dangerous whirlpools. Also a female monster, she is like an enormous bladder with flippers, and she swallows a huge amount of sea water and then vomits it back out to form whirlpools that cause ships to sink. It is assumed that Charybdis eats the sailors, and the ships too.

'BETWEEN SCYLLA AND CHARYBDIS'

The Greek legend is that these two monsters live on either side of a strait, or narrow channel of water, and work in partnership. Sailors who steer their ship away from one will be caught by the other. So, the expression "to be between Scylla and Charybdis" means to be caught between two bad things and unable to avoid either of them.

MERMAID

MERMAID

OTHER NAMES: Merman.

FACT OR FICTION: Fiction.

DESCRIPTION: About the same size as a human but half woman (or man) and half fish. The human half (from the waist up) of the mermaid is that of a beautiful young woman with long hair, and the bottom half is long and scaly with a fish-like tail.

WHERE THEY LIVE: Under the sea, sometimes in beautiful palaces of coral, decorated with pearls.

POWERS: Some mermaids can sing beautiful songs that lure human men into the sea. Powerful swimmers. One Chinese mermaid was said to be able to create priceless pearls from her tears.

WEAKNESSES: Having fish tails, they can only survive in the sea and not venture onto land.

DIET: Fish.

OTHER: Seeing a mermaid is sometimes thought of as an omen of bad luck, especially to sailors, for whom it often means the approach of bad weather.

A MERMAID is half-woman, half-fish, usually beautiful with long shining hair, and has a lovely singing voice. The word "mermaid" is made up of the words "mere" (which was the Old English word for "sea") and "maid," meaning a young woman.

MERFOLK

There are many stories of mermaids from around the world. Mermen—half-men, half-fish—are less often talked about, but do appear in some stories.

Both mermaids and mermen can be serious trouble for human beings. Mermaids are quite vain and spend time combing their hair and admiring their own reflection. Often you hear a mermaid's voice before you see her. They sing beautifully, and their song, once heard, will haunt you forever.

People are fascinated by mermaids, and mermaids are fascinated by people, and that's where the danger is. The typical mermaid story tells of a man falling in love with a mermaid who takes him down to her home under the sea—where, of course, he drowns. Some say that mermaids are simply not very smart and don't realize that humans can't breathe under water, while others believe that mermaids actually delight in charming foolish men and leading them to their doom. But mermaids can also fall in love with human men and follow them onto land. Obviously then, things become very difficult for a mermaid because she can't walk. Different stories tell of mermaids desperately trying to hide their tails, or even striking a terrible bargain with some magician so that they can walk, but only at the cost of extreme pain. In any case, these love affairs never end well and often lead to the death of the mermaid.

AN UNCONVINCING SCIENTIFIC EXPLANATION

Scientists have attempted to explain mermaid legends by saying that what the sailors actually saw was a seal, sea cow, or, more likely, a manatee. These gentle, slow-moving water mammals do have tails and do sometimes sit on rocks and watch passing ships, but there the resemblance ends. They are gray with big snouts and tiny, far apart eyes. It's hard to believe that many sailors through the ages could have mistaken them for beautiful mermaids.

GHOST SHIP

THERE ARE TWO KINDS of ghost ships—those that sail the seas with a crew of ghosts, and those that are found drifting with not a soul on board, and no sign of where the crew or passengers went. Seeing either kind of ghost ship is considered to be extremely unlucky.

GHOST SHIP

OTHER NAMES: Phantom ship.

FACT OR FICTION: The type of ghost ship with a crew of ghosts is fiction. But the type of ghost ship that is discovered sailing with no crew is fact.

DESCRIPTION: Usually just a regular-looking ship but sometimes they can be surrounded by an eerie ghostly light.

WHERE THEY LIVE: At sea.

POWERS: They don't actually have any special powers, but seeing one is a portent of doom.

FAMOUS GHOST SHIPS: The *Flying Dutchman* (see next page), the *Caleuche* (a mythical ghost ship from Chile), the *Lady Lovibond* (a ship wrecked in 1748, which appears off the coast of Kent in England every 50 years), the *Eliza Battle* (an American paddle steamer that caught fire at the end of the nineteenth century, which appears now and then in flames as a warning of disaster), the *Marie Celeste* (see next page), the *Carroll Deering* (a cargo ship that ran aground in 1921 and was found completely abandoned with no sign of crew).

HAUNTED SHIPS WITH A CREW OF GHOSTS

The most famous of this type of ghost ship is the *Flying Dutchman*. This ship eternally sails the seas, appearing suddenly and silently mid-ocean. If another ship tries to communicate, its sailors will reply, sending messages to people who are long dead. One legend is that the captain, or possibly the whole crew, once committed a terrible crime and are sailing the oceans forever as punishment. Another story is that the captain was once trying to sail the ship around the Cape of Good Hope in terrible winds. He swore that he would be eternally damned if he didn't get around the Cape that night. The ship was lost and doomed to carry out his threat forever. Many sailors have seen the ship, including the future King George V of England who supposedly saw it off the coast of Australia in 1880.

SHIPS WITH NO CREW

The most famous of these is the *Marie Celeste*. This merchant ship was found in the Atlantic Ocean on December 4, 1872. The ship was clean and in good condition, the sails were hoisted, and the ship was making good speed towards Gibraltar. There was enough food and water for six months. The belongings of the crew and passengers were all untouched. However, there was not a single person on board. There was no sign of violence or a struggle. One lifeboat was missing, but no one who had been on the ship was ever seen or heard from again.

GLOSSARY

Aboriginal: of or relating to a member of any of the native people of Australia

Cape of Good Hope: a cape on the Atlantic coast of South Africa

Carnivore: a meat-eating animal

Cavity: a hollow or unfilled space

Estuary: an arm of the sea at the lower end of a river

Figment: something imagined or made up

Mythology: a collection of myths dealing with the gods/goddesses of a particular people

Nymph: a goddess in an old legend that is represented as a beautiful young girl living in a forest, meadow, mountain, or water

Oarfish: the longest bony fish in the sea

Portent: a sign or warning of a coming event

Prehistoric: of, relating to, or existing in the time before written history

Primitive: of or relating to the earliest age or period

Prosperous: having or showing success or financial good fortune

Strait: a narrow channel connecting two large bodies of water

Sturgeon: any of various large and long fishes having a thick skin covered with rows of bony plates

Supernatural: of or relating to an existence of something beyond the observable universe

Tourist attraction: a place of interest for travelers

Undulating: to move in waves

Whirlpool: water moving rapidly in a circle with a hollow in the center

Please visit our website, www.garethstevens.com. For a free color catalog of all our high-quality books, call toll free 1-800-542-2595 or fax 1-877-542-2596.

Library of Congress Cataloging-in-Publication Data

Cox, Barbara.
Wicked waters / by Barbara Cox and Scott Forbes.
   p. cm. — (Creepy chronicles)
Includes index.
ISBN 978-1-4824-0264-3 (pbk.)
ISBN 978-1-4824-0265-0 (6-pack)
ISBN 978-1-4824-0262-9 (library binding)
1. Sea monsters — Juvenile literature. 2. Monsters — Juvenile literature. I. Title.
QL89.C69 2014
001.9—dc23

First Edition

Published in 2014 by
Gareth Stevens Publishing
111 East 14th Street, Suite 349
New York, NY 10003

Produced for Gareth Stevens by Red Lemon Press Limited
Concept and Project Manager: Ariana Klepac
Designer: Emilia Toia
Design Assistant: Haylee Bruce
Picture Researcher: Ariana Klepac
Text: Scott Forbes (Forest, Castle, Desert), Barbara Cox (all other text)
Indexer: Trevor Matthews

Images: Every effort has been made to trace and contact the copyright holders prior to publication. If notified, the publisher undertakes to rectify any errors or omissions at the earliest opportunity.

Art Archive: 25 br in box
Bridgeman Art Library: 2 tl and b, 3 tr, 11 br, 12 t, 13 tr in box and b (Fairy Art Museum, Tokyo, Japan), 17 t, 18 b, 18 front, 20 t, 21 bl in box, 22 t, cover and 23 tr in box and b, 26 tl,
Getty Images: 5 inset, 6 tl, 7 bl in box, 8 b in box, 14 br in box. Granger Collection: 19 br in box, 24 t and cl,
iStockphoto: other images as follows:
cross stitches 6, 8, 11, 15, 23, 26; grunge borders 7, 16, 19, 25; hands 7, 8, 16, 19, 25; stick borders 6, 18, 24, 26.
Martin Hargreaves: 8 t, 15 tr.
Shutterstock: all other images

KEY: t = top, b = bottom, l = left, r = right, c = center

Printed in the United States of America

CPSIA compliance information: Batch #CW14GS: For further information contact Gareth Stevens, New York, New York at 1-800-542-2595.

Gareth Stevens
Publishing